The Liskeard Poets
Out of the Box

Selected poems from this mutable but long-standing group who come together, from all parts of SE Cornwall and beyond, to work their poetry in Liskeard.

The term 'out of the box' is used during our workshop sessions to denote the time when the poet may speak, after discussion of their work by the rest of the group.

This collection was independently selected by the author and poet Jenny Alexander from poems submitted by the members of the Liskeard Poetry Group

The Liskeard Poets

Out of the Box

ISBN 978-1-909936-24-9

Copyright © 2017 The Liskeard Poets.
Each poet as named has asserted his or her right under the Copyright, Designs and Patents Act 1988 to be identified as the author of their named work

All rights reserved. This book or any portion thereof may not be reproduced or used in any manner whatsoever without the express written permission of the publisher except for the use of brief quotations in a review.

Paperback Edition 2017 Pendown Publishing
Cornwall, United Kingdom

Set in 12pt Calibri
Printed by Lightning Source

www.pendownpublishing.co.uk

Cover: PP designs

OUT of the BOX

The Liskeard Poets and Poems

Anna Chorlton   5
  Water Marks
  Winter Woods
  From Me to You (Downderry Beach)

Ian Craft   10
  Roses and Tulips
  Hoepker's 9/11
  Unashamed Desire in a Restaurant

Clare Dwyer   15
  A Dark Remembered Rose
  Not Just A Cornish Landmark
  Falling Into Darkness
  Peter Sansom's Vest

Ann Foweraker   20
  Judging by the Cover – a villanelle
  Shadowing
  How to Grow Poppies
  Subtractions
  Sonnet on keeping a lover secret

Jan Hare   26
  Teresa
  Landmark
  The Horses are Galloping

Margot Hartley   31
  Another Sunday
  Colour
  Southport December 2014
  Booly Beach

Poets and poems continued ...

Mary Harvey   36
Mandarin Sun
Adders
The Black Rose
Early June

Paddy Hunter   40
Lanteglos
Michaelmas
Midsummer Madness

Meriel Kitson   44
Matilda
Sequence

Victoria Nelson   47
Trio Sonnet
Dancing with shadows

Mike Rockliffe-King   50
Visitors
Letter to the CEO of the Meduse Cruise Line
Words in Progress
Lotte. Henada Woods. November
Fracture

John Whelan   56
The Voyeur
Summer's Joy – a sestina

Chris Woolf   60
When kissing is in season
Lilies
Telling me Softly
Jessie
Ask Your Eyes

About Jenny Alexander   66
About The Liskeard Poetry Group   67

Anna Chorlton

I have enjoyed writing poetry for fifteen years. I write about my emotional response to family life and to Bodmin Moor where I live.

Water Marks

Wenna water spirit, careful, subtle,
doesn't feel a threat
from commoner farmers grazing summer fields,
chequering the heather with horses, cows and wool,
slurping her ponds with coarse bearded tongues.

Wenna frolics over a tor staked by engine houses,
bound by rings of Bronze Age dwellings,
forced to lie amidst a fly-tipped mine.

Wenna is reflection, chimney pillars
perched on watery shafts,
the song of the sky on the surface,
her exhibit unnoticed,
repeating in concealed time.

Wenna doesn't feel the threat
of miners clutching tools
wedging granite to split,
years on, quarry fills trucks for the docks,
of the Cornishman's pride turned away.

Wenna doesn't see the threat
of a passing car with instructions to take one stone,
return for another.

"Perhaps a millstone for your mosaic yard?"
"Why not a standing stone, or a King's burial mound?
Drive over my reed thread skirts with traction wagons,
lorries, quads and motorcycles."

Wenna counts on endurance of history;
moor laced with cairns, mines and settlements,
seen in splendour from the air. Birds become her assets,
nesting in the foliage, mosses and reed shelters,
singing sound jewels above the valleys.

Threat doesn't come from carving up of moor land sides,
from thieves or kids, villages or Duchy.
Wenna is threat, she swells beneath earthen drapes,
rushes through mine shafts, surges in dark pools,
leaches in ponds, marsh fields and leats.

Wenna is grip-penetrating the moor.
Armoured with reeds she falls
into springs, moving life into four sedating rivers.
Threatening as winter weather, bossed by water,
the wind from the sea and the weighted fog.

Through the defunct shafts Wenna chuckles,
 nibbles on cement the stone mason poured.
It snows and rains as Wenna's strength expands,
she rushes over hedge walls
toward front doors and is diverted into sinking pools.

Winter Woods

A woman loiters
hair pulled in a
band of satin
a long back

a man rides up
adjusts his hat
bright amused eyes
waits for a response

she hastens to the stable
leads out a mare
mounts
trots on into

winter woods
the view expansive
a woodpecker, a deer
hooves scrunch stones

a shared expectation
feet curl in damp boots
horses step together
he leans to caress her

edges of the woodland
air is wet
a hill of black trees
bark of cow

a departing sun
birdsong
a feeling of alliance.

From Me to You (Downderry Beach)

You doze beside a picnic hamper,
feeding the remnants of a marriage.
Sun compliments cheeks, arms, frown
of a woman, waiting beside the ocean.
Whispers, "As you sleep, children wade."

Mother looks into a thoughtful sea.
Buffeted by newspapers, clothed.
She pushes her heels into sand,
calculating the weight
in a family of gulls.

Loitering, I skim eyes over her same sea,
force my focus back to now as protector.
Hold your young body as you recoil from the soar
of first waves. Feel uneasy with time.
Wonder, with whom are you?

Say, "Baby, your childhood comes as I age."
Feel, an irrevocable loss,
of youth submerging within time
and see amongst the spiral of life your beginning,
alone in fragile joy, you stand on life's periphery.

Ian Craft

Enidblytonjohnkeatsstephenspenderwilfredowen
adrianhenrirogermcgoughbrianpattenlawrencefer
linghettisylviaplathleonardcohen(ee)cum(mings)
tseliotbobdylankatetempestanonanonanon

love lust loss death dying getting old life sun moon the usual.

Thank you Don Nunes

Roses and Tulips
(soldier's notebook: machine-gun course 1914)

Who is this man
Who, in his notes,
Learned to assemble & dissemble,
Learned to kill but not be killed,
And in the margins drew roses and tulips?

Who is this man
Rising to the call,
Whose two lips were a better target for kisses,
Who flirted with death
And grew flowers in the margins of history?

Who is this man
Who left his Cornish home
To dig in foreign fields,
To firmly plant his gun
And fire?

The fact he named the parts and used them,
Offered his life,
Lived and returned,
Is not our concern.
The simple fact we should record
Is that he drew roses and tulips in the margins.

Hoepker's 9/11
(Thomas Hoepker, Magnum photographer, took an iconic photo of the Twin Towers)

Like a corner of some Breughel painting,
they are gathered there
breaking bread and laughing
whilst the world is torn apart.

The clear blue sky, the postures,
the smiles
say this is life
whilst, unnoticed, plumes Death.

The details demand our attention:
the statemented hair,
the tattoo, the shorts,
the stretched bare midriff,

the red-trimmed trainers,
the red-checked shirt,
the red bike,
the blood unseen,

the sidewalk's stain
almost unnoticed.
The stain in the sky
almost the same.

The shades, the shadows,
the bended knees
are what takes our focus.
We lose ourselves in the detail.

And yet these mundane images are
the life contained in this small corner
of many small corners
where Death holds no dominion.

And then the eye turns and returns
to the plume and the building
and if you look closely you could believe
you see someone falling.

Unashamed Desire in a Restaurant

A desert sun
shines from her skin, black
as an ocean pebble,
pure and polished.

Clothed in turquoise
like the sea,
diamonds rippling
around her neck.

A liquid tongue
speaks an alien language,
slipping between Gaul & Arabia
and her lips.

This grey old man
longs
for the white of your smile
and the deep dark pools of your eyes.

Clare Dwyer

I still remember the first poem which appealed to me aged five and I have been reading and writing poetry ever since (nearly sixty years!). Some of my favourites are Coleridge's Conversation Poems; 'In a Lime Tree Bower' and 'Frost At Midnight'. It is the intimacy of these which I try to capture in my own poetry

A Dark Remembered Rose.

The rosebush in my garden flowers still,
Each bud dark red in secret perfection.

I saw you last in that box
lined with smooth white wedding satin.
Your face drawn, fleshless,
Your hair still black, sleek
as a well fed witch's cat.
In that box I laid a rose,
grown from a little slip,
 your garden to mine.
It's dark slender elegance
the essence which had been you.

We buried you on a drear December day
of biting cold and drenching sky.
In the cold church we sang hymns thinly
voices cracked with weeping;
then the graveyard where
red Devon clay lay raw
beside the grave my eyes refused to see.

We held your wake,
not with soft sad sighs,
but tales of you and loving laughter
knitting your past in memories.
And in the garden
I saw on your rose
a single frostbitten bud.

Not Just A Cornish Landmark

All I wanted was to be, to remain, myself
with no label of victim, patient, survivor,
but nothing was straightforward.
On the switchback of surgeries, treatment, infection
self fell away into fatigue, appointments, waiting.
Now I am all those things,
I cannot see myself at all.

I still notice the splash on primrosed banks,
the smoke of blue bells through the trees,
how delicate the drapery of new leaves
and the long surf-topped waves
against the shouldering cliffs;
but all this is backdrop
it is no longer my landscape.

My landscape has bleak grey tiredness
which no sleep relieves.
Exhaustion bogs each limb,
drowns thought, smothers self.
Escape is slow dragging footsteps,
the future mist-shrouded,
the path so very steep.

Falling Into Darkness

Summer's slow death has come,
colours fade from the garden;
leaves, their work done,
drift, some slow, aimless;
others scurry around
in a hurry to be - somewhere.
Damp is in the air,
spider webs cling to every
leaf and cane, brown earth is exposed.
Darkness stretches fingers
deep into morning and picks
at the edges of afternoon
to pull the night closer,
answering nature's need
for the long sleep of winter

Peter Sansom's Vest

(Seagulls and teapots: the contemporary idiom;
in Writing Poems by Peter Sansom p36/37)
'it is clear I think why we don't find more
vests and settees in contemporary poetry'

The broken sofa stood
at right angles to the sea
just below the tide line
as if washed up by some
running storm.
Perhaps the hope was
that it might float out to sea
on an improbably high tide
to be the momentary resting place
for some passing mermaid
in need of a quiet space to perch.

The corners were looped about
with shredded, frayed fragments of cloth
and the ends of the arms where,
 many hands, many times,
had pushed down to take
the strain off knees.
From great tears bulged
mounds of foam,
stained brown with age.
There was still, faintly,
the bold geometric pattern
that had once seared eyes
with electric jags of blue
against the now indeterminate background.

And on one crazily angled cushion hung
the myriad shards (sorry, shreds) of Peter Sansom's vest.

Ann Foweraker

Since I was eight or nine poetry has written me, rather than the other way round. Simple rhyme and rhythm became existential teenage angst and matured into, well, a gallimaufry. Heart on sleeve, layered intensity, love to despair, strict form or free – whatever catches my heart or eye can trigger a poem – yet after fifty odd years (twenty with the Liskeard Poets) and though now I also write novels - it's still poetry that writes me.

Judging by the Cover – a villanelle

I really thought I could read him like a book,
it was to be so easy to make him mine -
it was just a matter of the perfect hook.

Then when he gave me that certain kinda look
I knew everything would be just fine,
I really thought I could read him like a book.

When he said, he didn't think I ought to cook;
instead I took him expensively to dine
It was just a matter of the perfect hook.

When my friends told me they thought he was a crook
I believed they were just spinning me a line,
I really thought I could read him like a book.

I gave him everything, and he took
while telling me, everything was just fine,
it was just a matter of the perfect hook.

Dear reader, his cover's worth a second look
but beware, read beyond his opening line.
I really thought I could read him like a book
it was just a matter of the perfect hook.

Shadowing

I am gathering wood in the top field,
my back bent, I stoop from twig to twig,
wrapped in thick layers against the icy
north-easterly that clips the ridge
and slices down the slope.

The goats have settled further along,
near the place I found the loom-weights.
As I move towards them I step
into a silence, where the wind
skips over my head and sun warms.

Then I see her; shadowing me.
And I know she's left the baby in the hut
her loom stripped of its thread, her man away.
Shapelessly wrapped, she stoops
her back bent, twig by twig, gathering wood.

How to Grow Poppies

For flowers in abundance
row after row, whole
landscapes turned crimson, first
turn the soil.
Digging trenches works well.

Poppies thrive in open spaces,
the removal of trees and other shade
is recommended.

Fertilize well, blood and bone is best.
Water in, a long winter of rain at least,
and leave ... nature will do the rest.

Subtractions

From the age of three
numbers danced for her,
times-tables flew to thirteen
before she was even seven,
algebra, algorithms
fractions and percentages
were her friends.

Given two facts she could
calculate when events happened.
Dates and times gave
her memories meaning,
more than the smell of almonds,
the touch of peach skin
or taste of lavender, breathed in.

And words were for ordering,
making neat in reports
with every grammatical
rule obeyed perfectly
and every word
instantly spelled
correctly.

But now, the 'when' escapes her,
time has developed holes
and days mutated, while
words start to wander,
lost as much as the photo
she found today and lost again
before she could show me.

Even now, it's not how you spell it
and it's not the numbers
that are the problem,
but the remembering to
carry-one-on, functioning
within snap-shots of time,
worrying about everything.

Sonnet on keeping a lover secret

Always find a new lover with the same
name as your partner or husband or wife,
it makes life easier, for the main aim
is to prevent slips and consequent strife.
Never tell lies unless you really must,
don't trust your memory, always include
an element of truth that can be pushed
to cover an unexplained interlude.
Always be sure to delete, and empty
the bin, don't be tempted to keep any
thing, word, token, all may find you guilty,
but even one could be one too many.
And never, ever, no matter what comes
write of your lover in one of your poems.

Jan Hare

I have always loved words but this became a passionate affair when I retired from suburbia to Cornwall. I revel in my new relationship with time and the impact of Cornwall. The flash of inspiration, capturing the right words to fit the sadness or joy, squirreling words in my notebook, learning, unwrapping the poetry present - DELIGHT!

Teresa

I spelt your name with an 'h'
but there wasn't one.
You didn't mind and now it doesn't matter.
So much shouldn't matter.
But it does.

You painted blue with yellow spots around your windows.
Had an outrageous coloured glass chandelier.
You smiled such warmth with trembling hands,
unfathomable eyes.
I hugged your thin body
feeling the fragility you rarely mentioned.

You liked Status Quo.
I only know because it played at your funeral.
I met your friends from junior school
crowded in your kitchen.
Staunch in their love for you.
Reminiscing about a Teresa I didn't know.
Party girl. Teaser. Jester.

When I met you your shell was formed.
Lovely, lovely you but so, so sad somehow.
I wish I'd known you better.
What happened on your way here?
The here that is mine but not yours.

So much shouldn't matter.
But it does.

Landmark

The pair walk slowly.
She schoolgirl bloom,
he unsure in gangly new limbs.
Shy glances
words tumbling from stumbling lips.
So much to say to this new.

LOOK. Look at my new.
Trees the same
streets the same
feet the same,
but not hands.
Twice as large,
on fire as fingers brush.
Palms sweat.

The wood deepens, brambles snag.
She stumbles and he catches her
awkwardly.
Turns her to face him.
Brown eyes on blue.
Hoping. Questioning.
Ginger down on his lip.
Freckles.
Pulls me to him and
his lips touch mine.
Softly. Gently. Oh so softly.
Sweet as the sweetest thing.
And my world kicks out of kilter.

Cornwall in June.
There it is - Jacks Wood.
Smaller than I remember.
Still as precious.
My lips blasted since by 60 years of life
sometimes still feel the wonder of
that kiss of incomparable softness.
Was it a landmark for him I wonder?

The Horses are Galloping

Stooping low, weeding,
through the earth I feel the sound ....
the horses are galloping.

Run to field edge, cross the lane,
stand at branch framed gate.
The horses are galloping.

Field rises. Sun sets. Eyes blaze.
Round and round their silhouettes race.
Black on gold.
The horses are galloping.

Hooves pound. Manes stream. Hearts fire.
Push to lung limit.
The horses are galloping.

Two buzzards on fence posts
calling each other.
We watch.
Do they share my breathless wonder?

I scream for human- and animal-kind
who cannot be this free.
As nature intended.

The horses are galloping.
I shout my joy to the wind.

Margot Hartley

"I can see poetry in this work" - and the tide rose in my soul at this comment on my jewellery 30 years ago. The blood red patina I create on my copper jewellery defines my work; this sanguine core wants to flow through my poetry. I begin with an empty sheet of metal, an empty page, and design the piece, scribe the pattern, cut the shape, file the unwanted edges. Then fret intricate detail, bond metal on metal, word on word, hammer the form, polish and polish, until what was latent is now fashioned as poem or jewellery.

Another Sunday

Good Morning Sunday
I am remembering Marbella
the warm sun
the golden sand
you in the sea
floating about
me pebble hunting furiously.
It's biting here
this day,
that wind
vicious
as it seeps through windows
doors and floors.
I want to stay in bed
let Sunday bounce off
with its roasted families and friends.
But I'm part of that roast for once
A gravy of folk chit-chatting their holiday plans
dissecting ailments
elongated like summer dusk shadows.
I can shut the door on loneliness
leave it panting.
Poor thing all alone
waiting for the key to eat the lock
claim its victim
shape the soul with emptiness.
Alas,
Another speck of honour gone
Enjoy your Sunday roast!

Colour

The colour of your dress
explodes intense crystalized blue,
moving the sky to blush.
The colour of your coat performed
a play of floral words;
shooting sentences through tamed silence.

The colour of your smile sent
a rose of passion
framed by even ivory teeth,
that heat a blood red pulse
rising high as a spring tide.

The colour this palette keeps
a grey slate mixed with olive green
waiting for shafting sunlight to reap
opalized river ripples

The colour sunshine opens
the autumn door
leaving permanence
rich in ambered décor.
An opulent feast;
Red, vermillion, gold, orange, aging brown
and desperate green clinging on,
refusing to let summer end in deadly song.

The colour perfume leaks,
rich with fruit, and leaf mould
a spectrum speech blasts the senses
with the herald of winter sleep
of barren, dark sombre days
where trees silhouette their friendship
in angled ways.

Southport December 2014

Here is my take on Southport thus far:
Southport is a Victorian relic.
Trees line Lord street
twinkling in their splendour.
Northerners are loud
their conversation blasts through the wind
its content the same
about her tits and arse
good enough to shit on!

Did Gormleys boys echo this?
As they stand naked on Crosby sands
looking dolefully out to sea.
A sea so grey and cruel
my toe couldn't test its temptation.
We decorated number 21
put a Santa's hat upon his head
Merry Christmas Mr Gormley's barnacled boys.

Today we will venture in the pine
to see nature's treasure
Squirrel Nutkin, red divine.
And later the parents
The family tree, hmm....
slightly nervous feelings flutter in.
Wish me luck dear friends.

Booly Beach

Tracks from different folk
mark the mud,
deep and slippy,
sometimes I wobble.
Finally Booly
lies waiting:
surf creeping in and out.
Pebbles stack small mountains
grey and white,
and grey and yellow decorate.
The weed
the sea washed in
glistens without a sun ray.
The cliffs,
shoulder to shoulder
weep water,
sprinkling a false rain
for pippets quenching.
The sea roll,
grey and brown
with white surf fizzing,
tempting enough to paddle.
Yes I let the icy lace
cover naked feet
that sink in Tai Chi pose.

Lovely Booly always silent
But for the groans,
the waves hold ready to explode,
against sand, pebble, rock
I live for it,
the dance the water gives.

Mary Harvey

Since 1959, Mary Harvey has lived on the edge of Bodmin Moor; the Cornish landscape has influenced much of her writing – a contrast to her native East Anglia. The use of language, and languages, has always been a source of delight.

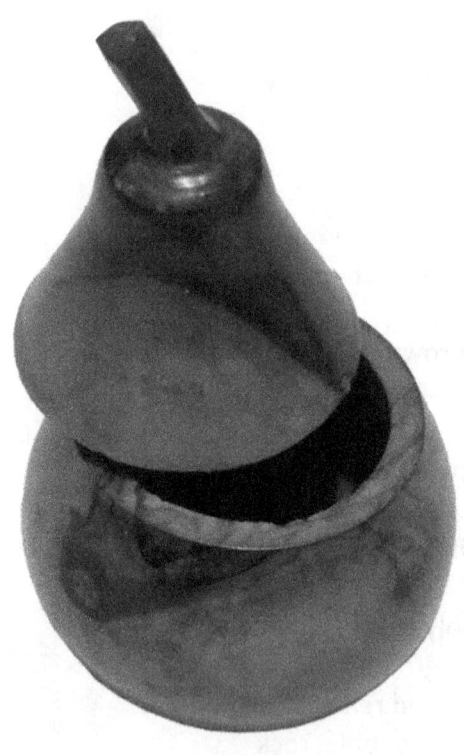

Mandarin Sun

With the lilt of the light – a zesty dawn,
lemon slices streak the cirrus clouds
to polish the lime-green laurels,
pinpoint boles of beech.

A tangerine burns in a wide, blue bowl,
light expands to heat, at noon –
shrivels leaves and swallows dew.

A shiver of dusk defers to the west,
its citrus sunset, wild-fire sky,
slowly, wholly doused by the dark.

Adders

Sinuous as stoats, a flicker in the ling
or stark on granite stones, like uncoiled springs,
the adders lifted fine fastidious heads.
Renascent from their sleep, they sipped the sun,
sensual, ingesting slow its April warmth.
Rising like sap, they bared stiletto fangs,
then, quiet as suspirations, they withdrew
slipped silently beneath the bracken frond,
young, unfolded fingers, like a child.
Alone, I saw the passing of such power
and felt disquiet on such a peaceful day.

The Black Rose

Out of my deep dream sleep
a full, black rose,
perfectly formed, but stark
on a leafless stem.
Next day, the dream translated into song –
symbol of sorrow for Sibelius,
bleak, in his northern land,
a black rose, drained of light.

Then, I thought of Frans Hal
to whom Van Gogh ascribed
twenty-seven shades of black;
petal by petal, gathered to one flower,
rejection, failure, longing, absence, grief –
twenty-seven sorrows mass and furl
into a dark and elegiac whole,
out of the shapeless mystery of pain.

Early June

This is the first scene of the second Act
in the drama of seasons;
the may is a dazzling divertissement,
a cascading dance
to follow the blackthorn's fragile blooms
that, hesitant, moved into sloe, quick sloe.

Rinsed by the pounding showers,
bluebells turn pale and droop,
as the purple gauntlet thrust
of emerging foxgloves
open freckled centres
to the delving of the bees.

After the feeding frenzy of the Spring,
fledglings flush and stagger on the air,
turn topsy-turvy in the high, fresh beech,
augment the clamorous chorus of first light.

With a darkening swish
the heavy curtain falls,
Constable-green on the second Act

Paddy Hunter

I have always loved reading poetry, from 'A Child's Garden of Verses' through to Seamus Heaney and the poets of today. I have been a member of the Liskeard Poetry Group for almost ten years, and it has been a delight to discover and learn so much more through writing and working with the group.

Lanteglos

On the cliff path a wind,
sudden and bitter, caught us
turned us back.
Buffeted, heads bowed,
we followed the path
downward.

But on the incline I saw,
half-hidden in the hedgerow,
just one violet,
and on its petals
just one raindrop
sea-salty as a tear,
vibrant as hope:

and thought of her wry smile
world-wise as Malala's,
possessed of a certainty
beyond their scarce years
and my weary reasoning
that, despite everything,
all will be well.

Michaelmas

They stitch daisies, the two old friends,
sat in late sun beneath the apple trees.
Grey heads bent, together they border
a tablecloth with garlands of flowers:
each mauve petal held with a slip stitch,
each flower finished with a knot of gold.
Sharp as their memories the silver needles
dip in and out of creamy linen,
as deftly they pattern past riches
onto the plain fabric of the day.
Long gone now, yet in my garden
in unseasonable heat, the murmur
of their voices falls soft as the lull of bees
that linger in the last of autumn's daisies.

Midsummer Madness

One day I will murder the man with the strimmer.
It should be the perfect crime, but if detected,
I shall claim self defence -
the man is armed and dangerous.
I will slip unseen amid the roses,
stalk him down beyond the sweet peas,
follow his machine's roar and the stench of petrol:
catch him where the daisies fly,
and the wild flowers lie dying.

A silent swipe of the scythe would do it,
but I am inclined to something more organic.
I will tangle him in bindweed,
smother him softly with thistledown
lay him on the compost heap on a bed of nettles
and cover him over with slain campion.

Nothing much will have changed with his passing -
It will just be a little quieter.

Meriel Kitson

I always loved reading poetry and, aged about 12, started writing awful rhyming couplets. I became bipolar in my teens and found writing poetry a way of struggling back into reality. Some were published by Somerville College, Oxford following a workshop day. The Liskeard poets have been immensely helpful to me at many levels.

Matilda

Working together
concentrating silently.
Her hands agile, petite, precise,
my hands strong, wrinkled, tremulous.

Concentrating silently,
positioning old photographs.
My hands strong, wrinkled, tremulous,
Sellotaping photos in place.

Positioning old photographs,
a goose landing on snow.
Sellotaping photos in place,
we talk about geese.

A goose landing on snow,
evocative of teenage angst.
We talk about geese,
facts for her, memories for me.

Evocative of teenage angst,
wings outspread.
Facts for her, memories for me,
working together.

Sequence

I learnt to swim in the sea,
felt the ebb and flow of tides.
I learnt to row on the sea,
against the ebb and flow of tides.
I learnt to sail through the sea,
with the ebb and flow of tides.
Now I walk on the quay,
watching the moon,
Vagrant mistress of the sea.

Victoria Nelson

Writing happens accidentally and what hits the paper surprises me as much as anyone else.

Trio Sonnet

I have three children; three of them have me.
My love divided? Undivided love
For Polly, William and dear Jonny B.
Uniquely accorded mother's love did prove
With tripping tears, with Polly's teenage tantrums
Scary as Will's night-time fears,
Dissolving, holding one another tight.
They will remain when I return to earth,
Post-partum parting, part-in-part insane,
I'll leave them as they left me at their birth
More quietly, theirs the turn to cry in pain.
But when my arms're too cold for warm embrace,
They'll see my love in one another's face.

Dancing with shadows

Be my Valentine, Death, shake the cloth of despair
I am raped by these years of emotions and fears
unshuckle me poisonous, slumberous pearls
woo this overhung, life-peppered rancid old girl

Be my Valentine……..spread the cloth of despair
slice my rare-raw to blackened rib sad-eyed flesh bare
pour the claret-red bubbles and tiramisu
unshuckle oblivion, let me soak through

Be my Valentine…….wipe the cloth of despair
draw me under: tira mi, tira mi, tira mi so'
feed me powdery pearls that release or renew
unshuckle oblivion, let me soak through

I am raped by these years of emotions and fears
seduce me, so willingly now, on your bier
There's no bitterness leaving, no liquor untapped
Be my Valentine, Death, tear the cloth of despair

Mike Rockliffe-King

Kick-started by an article 'Bright is the ring of words', I was inspired by a brilliant teacher who led me to John Donne and TS Eliot, to the Green Man and the Canterbury Tales. After copywriting, my life was re-booted by a Theatre Degree at Dartington - from which I tumbled into 20 years of Drama teaching. I still revel in the sheer power and beauty of words.

Visitors

Same every year.
They arrive unannounced,
all the way from Africa.
It is not until you hear their sun-girt wittering
you realise they're back,
nesting in familiar places.
And you learn the fate of one tagged senior
who didn't make it across Saharan wastes this time.

Reaching into the cat-food cupboard
I find that foragers have called again.
Chewed cardboard corners
and tiny hard black pellets
betray the raid.
I curse the lazy cats –
too domesticated
to protect their store of man-made fodder.

Some come with gifts of groceries and wine.
Others thrust tentative petrol-station flowers.
Others still bring noise and kids and cases.
All fill our space
like an occupying army.
All are welcome except for those that bully through our lanes
in shiny needless four-by-fours.

Letter to the CEO of the Meduse Cruise Line
(After Theodore Gericault – the Raft of the Meduse – 1819 oil on canvas – The Louvre)

I didn't mind the rough Biscay seas,
or the mixed up reservations.
I never missed my morning teas
nor the daily "Lifeboat Stations".

The fact the pool was out of bounds,
the promenade deck closed,
the entertainments – nasty sounds –
were just life's standard woes.

The dysentery that we all had
was neither here nor there.
The food was really worse than bad.
The waiters had long hair.

Our Captain was an all out lush,
the Navigator too.
But none of these things were the push
that decided me to sue.

No! The reason, dear Director,
that I have issued writs
is the émigré defector,
Le Compte de Chaumareix.

By the time we saw the Argus
the wine was all long gone.
Just fifteen souls remained of us,
barely hanging on.

Had the Admiralty Board
been thinking on their feet
they might have picked a better Lord
to command their Fleet!

Words in Progress

Be careful with these words,
please,
because the ink is barely dry.
Observe the present order
but be prepared for future change.
As ever, adjectives assemble in droves
to challenge and outdo the larger nouns
for primacy.
Layout sometimes
s
 t
  u
   mbles.
Commas can't always choose their perfect place,
and brackets (often) insinuate themselves.
Rhyming,
in the modern way,
cedes sensibly to driving rhythms
and the occasional elegant device.
Whilst form
from Acrostic
to Zen-fired Haiku
can beat the meaningful
into a well-shaped mess.

Lotte. Henada Woods. November

The Silver Cross is old,
but serviceable and well-maintained.
Lotte is,
unwillingly and plank-like,
strapped in and blanket-swathed
and instantly as we set off
she deems our progress agreeable.
One wheel squeals, of course,
but my plodding rhythm soothes us both.

At the wood edge
we resume our early education –
recognising leaves –
and in her pre-language world
the daily order of re-discovery must be a careful iteration.

By happenstance, the first is Fig,
then Oak; Hazel; Beech; Privet:
Laurel; Ash; Holly; Blackthorn; Ivy and,
improbably, a jungle-stand of tall Bamboo beyond our
reach.

Chittering squirrels draw our eyes.
We stop and stare until
they fly outside our view.
On, to search for fugitive sheep
foraging our wood.
And they are worth the wait
for unexpected wild agility
and solid baleful stare.

Slowed by the steep incline
(or Grandad's aching knees)
we halt again to admire anything
and catch a breath.
Then it's the homeward run that counts
as Lotte sleeps in Silver Cross and grand-parental care.

Fracture

If only.
If only there were a way.
If I could do
I would have done
and changed the laws of time-travel
and so, myself.

If only I could give a former me advice.
Write a sage letter.
Alter behaviours.
Prevent patterns.
Produce a better product.

But in the doubting dawning hours,
when faces are turned to the wall,
when regrets build a tidal wave,
when Krapp-like, the tapes are endlessly reviewed,
I know I would not
could not
have taken heed.

John Whelan

Born in Dublin 1952, I have reached my sell-by date and my best-before date is probably behind me. I very much hope my use-by date is a long way in the future. My Gaelic name is Sean O' Faolain, a name I am proud to share with the Irish short story writer. I enjoy poetry, it helps to keep my brain active.

The Voyeur

I spied on you French kissing,
In awe, enthralled, transfixed,
Your long tongue so delicate,
Flicked in and out precisely.
Chaotic never erotic,
Stealing your lovers nectar.
Blurred in motion,
Yet so still while hovering.
Within your iridescent breast,
Heart beats a thousand times a minute,
Wings flapping so fast, unseen.
Buzzing so loud,
A nest of bees.
You magic creature,
You tiny humming bird.

Summer's Joy – a sestina

Her name was Summer,
She was raised by the sea.
Long days allowed her time to run,
Often she stumbled and took a fall.
Unlike Snowy her faithful dog,
Always sure footed in soft sand.

Life sometimes is like running in sand,
Winter drags, Spring new life, flourishes in Summer.
One year for humankind, seven for a dog,
Madly rushing to the sea.
Four legged he will not fall,
No matter how crazy is the run.

So much fun to be had out on a run,
Calories burned by exercising in sand.
Avoiding the dunes, missing a fall,
Long, hot days the gift of Summer.
Time well spent by the sea,
By the lonely girl and her dog.

The White Alsatian dog,
Never walked would always run.
Loved to be taken to the sea,
The girl knew he loved the sand,
She was his master she was his Summer.
Soon it would be his Fall.

Winter cold would follow the Fall,
Life divided by seven for the dog.
He would never be forgotten by Summer,
All alone now on a run.
Her feet so hampered by the sand,
Then washed clean by the icy sea.

The girl then, now a woman, bought a house by the sea,
Summer's summer was now her fall.
Now much older she walks on the sand,
She has never forgot the white Alsatian dog.
Who madly, crazily would always run,
For him it never ended it was always Summer.

With his Summer by the sea,
He would run and never fall,
Snowy the white Alsatian dog lies hidden by the sand.

Chris Woolf

I have been writing poems to please myself and my friends, for about a quarter of a century. I write to capture events or feelings that, for me, have a particular charm or importance. Although I have a background in technical media, and could use cameras or audio recorders, I find writing works better. Mind you, words are crafty devices, with a life of their own, and a waywardness if not watched over - sometimes they need to be cuddled or even tempted with chocolate – but they are good company and can speak beautifully.

When kissing is in season

A brilliance
in the dappled
cloudscape
that is cotton grass
and purple heather -
on any day,
across the year,
it is the sunlight
of the moor.

A light
that shines
as bright in sleet,
as on a sultry
summer's afternoon
and hints
at all the heat
a furze-fire
brings.

So too,
its spines
are fierce -
but its sepals
are as soft
as spider silk,
and its petals part
erotically,
for every passing
humble bee.

Lilies

A still night,
and close.
The scent of lilies
in the ginger-jar
hangs heavy,
and the sultry air
itself
can hardly dare
to breathe.

The duvet
is flung wide,
the pillows
crumpled
into stones,
and sleep
long since became
your cruel,
deceitful
friend.

An owl
hunts noiselessly -
no wooing -
a moth
flies wordlessly
around the room -
and all is silence,
silence,
except the thud
of a petal
that drops
upon the bedroom floor.

Telling me Softly

It's filleted, of course.
The stinking guts
removed,
the head cut off
unceremoniously;
the backbone
stripped away
to just its imprint;
the tale cut short.

And she wraps it up
so carefully -
as if she's worried
that it's me
that might be soiled
by the taint
of what she whispers
in my ear,
one hand on my elbow

so delicately
that I almost miss
the bitter note,
the sour seaweed tang,
the distant storm
of scales that must have
showered in her hair,
and the pain
of sea-salt water
in her eyes.

Jessie

She has bought herself
a brand new coat –
cherry red.

Black or grey,
so very much more sensible,
her husband would have said.
A coat that you could wear again
to church and charity
and funerals.
Something practical
that would not show the dirt;
something that would go
with every dress and skirt
that she already had.
Something that would never
cause an eye to shine,
or put a knot or tangle
in thirty years
of marriage lines.

But now he's dead,
and she can sparkle
once again,
in cherry red.

Ask Your Eyes

If I can
I ask your eyes.

I tilt my head
a little
and look,
I hope unnoticed,

for that little stain
of tiredness
in the angles
of your cheeks,

for the lines
where corner-spiders
drag
their webs

or for the hint
of eyebrows pinching

before you flick
your glance to me
with its flash
of fireflies.

About Jenny Alexander

Jenny Alexander grew up in London but has lived all her adult life far from the capital, first in the Shetland Isles and, for the last thirty years, in Cornwall.

She has written scores of books for children and adults, both fiction and non-fiction, as well as magazine articles, poems, interactive CDRs and an Apple app, 'Get Writing!'

There's lots more information about Jenny's life, books and workshops on her website www.jennyalexander.co.uk

For this collection the Liskeard Poetry Group asked Jenny to select from 'up to six poems' submitted by each of the members of our group and we thank her for her diligent work in achieving this.

About The Liskeard Poetry Group

The Liskeard Poetry Group was founded about three decades ago by the poet Ann Gray, who was also the chairman of the group for many years. The group still has a small core of those early members, but many more have joined since then. Though it has met in many venues over time it has now settled into Stuart House – an Arts venue in an historic building on Barras Street in the middle of Liskeard, Cornwall.

The main function of the group is to provide a safe place where work can be shared and heard with constructive criticism being offered, only with the aim of supporting the development of the author's style, voice and quality of work.

A testament to the way it works is that each poet's voice is very distinctive within the group, even after many years of workshopping poems together.

As **The Liskeard Poets** we give readings at outside events, and have been regulars at the Port Eliot Festival, the Looe Literary Festival and the Bodmin Moor Poetry Festival. We are open to requests for performances at new events. We also work in collaboration with other local arts groups such as Vital Spark.

Our meetings are generally held on the second Monday of the month, at 4.15pm in Stuart House, Barras St. Liskeard, Cornwall. New members are welcome - please contact the secretary TheLiskeardPoets@yahoo.co.uk for up to date information.

Previous collections by The Liskeard Poets
Out of the Coombe
Lessons from the Camel School
WWI Poetry - pamphlet

www.ingramcontent.com/pod-product-compliance
Lightning Source LLC
Chambersburg PA
CBHW031423040426
42444CB00006B/693